30 DAYS OF COLORING BOOKS

FOR KIDS AND ADULTS

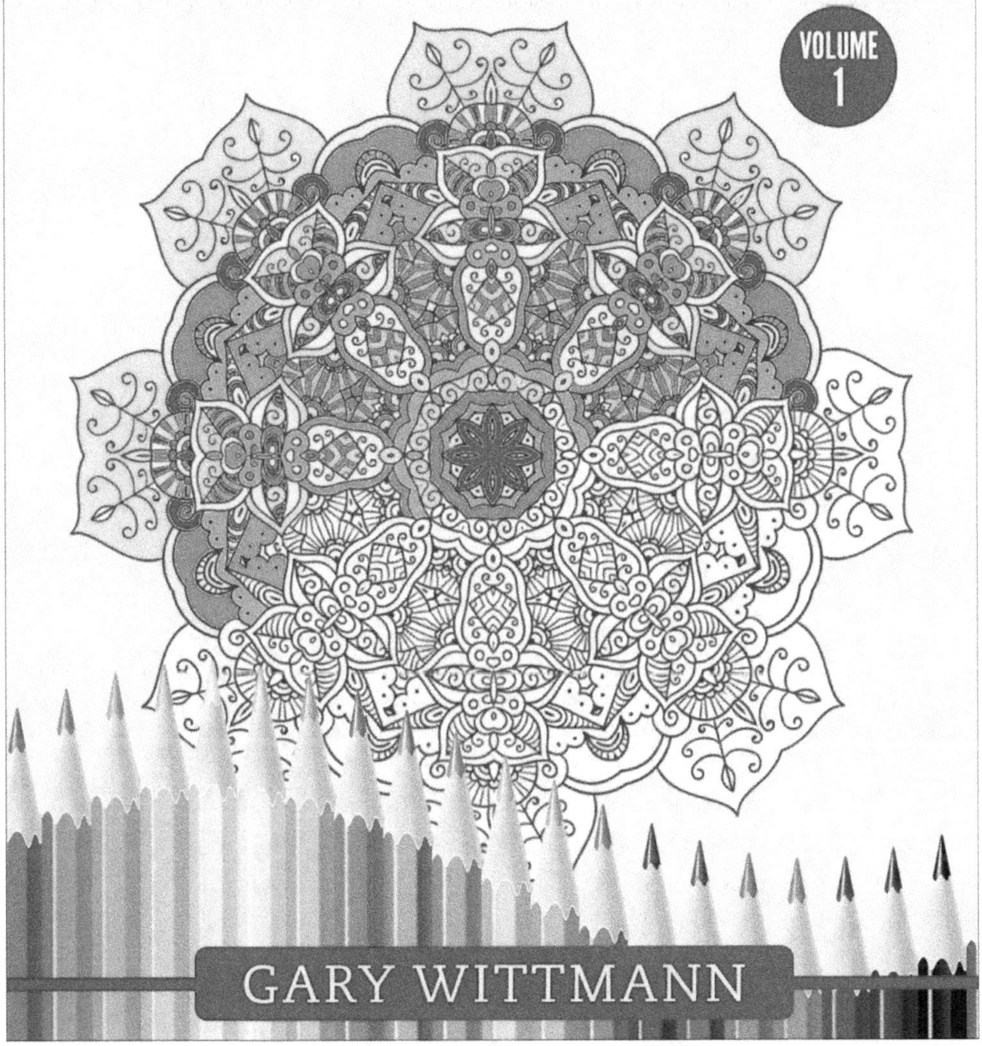

VOLUME 1

GARY WITTMANN

30 Days of Coloring Books

For Kids and Adults

By Gary Wittmann

30 Days of Coloring Books For Kids and Adults

By Gary Wittmann

Thanks for buying this ebook.   Sign up for the email to get news

about _____NEW_____ ebook that are free or low cost.

We will also send you new coloring pages.

http://www.getspecialbonus.com/coloringbooks/

Please join our facebook group

https://www.facebook.com/30DaysofColoringBooksForKidsandAdults/

https://www.pinterest.com/garywittmann/30-days-of-coloring-books-for-kids-and-adults/

https://twitter.com/30dayscolorbook

Instruction

I remember growing up and coloring at the kitchen table. Yes, Mom would hang them of the refrigerator. You can do that too. That feeling can be regained by coloring these pictures.

Let your mind drift into the pictures and you will feel yourself relax and having a stress free calm feeling come over you.

SUPPLIES

The coloring pages in this book are fairly intricate, so they're best suited to colored pencils or ink pens; however, you should feel free to use any medium you wish.

I've also included two intentionally blank pages (in the back of the book) for you to cut out and use behind the page you're working on. (Placing a blank sheet of paper behind the coloring page will protect the pages that follow from indentations and ink bleed.)

Happy Coloring and look for future coloring books.

Gary Wittmann

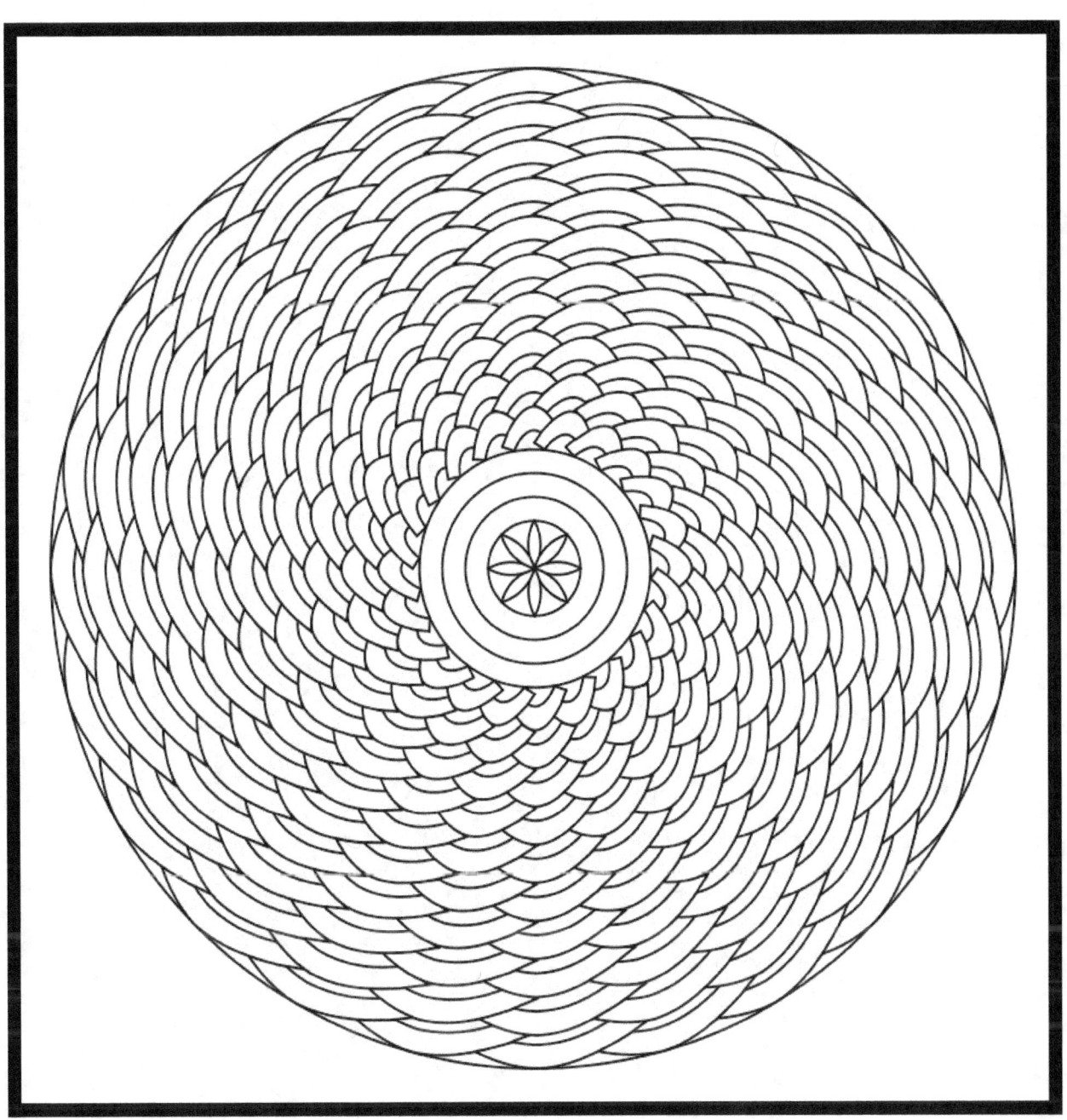

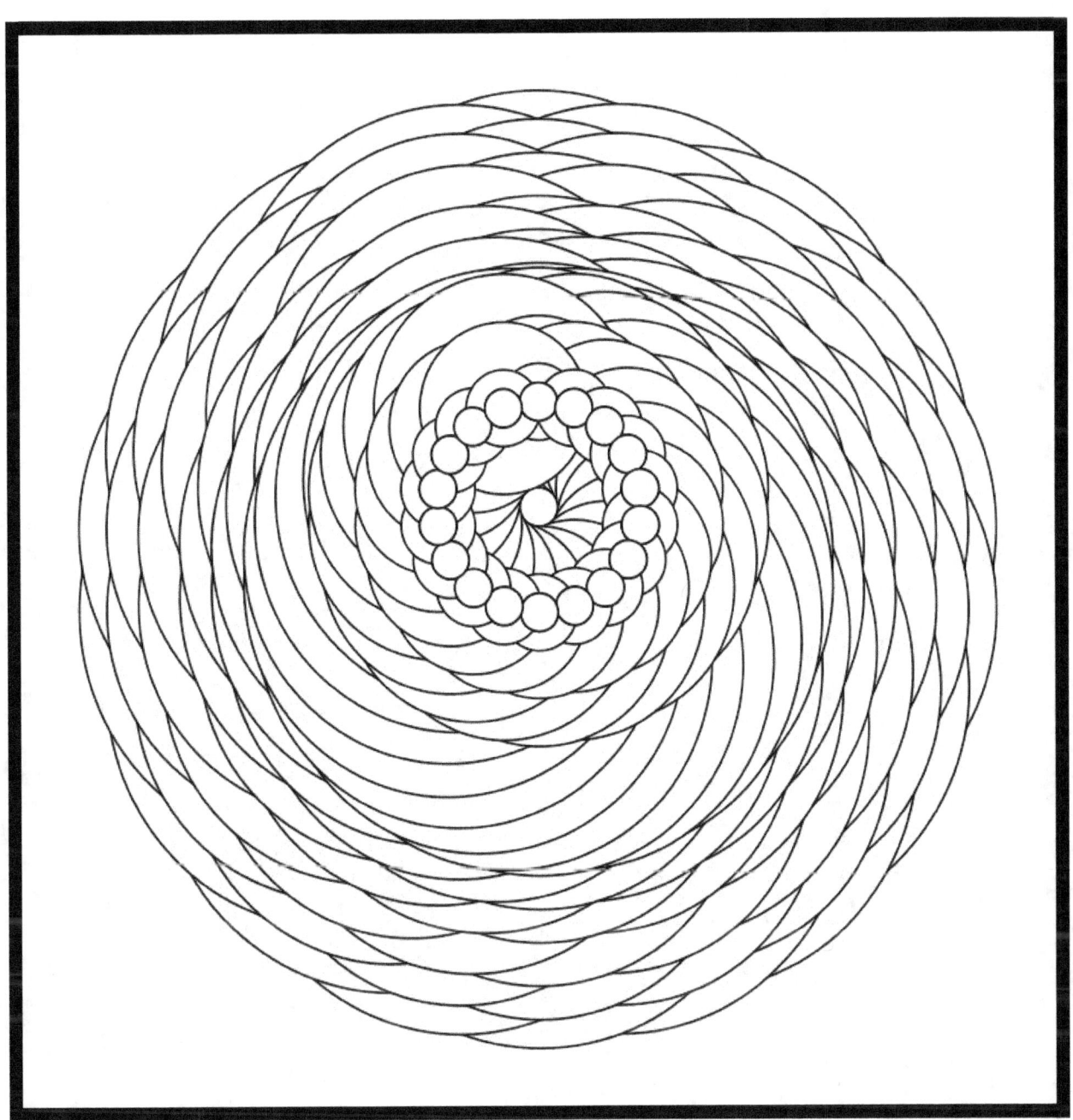

Again Thank you   if you could take a few minutes to give a review it will help others to find the series of Coloring Books by Gary Wittmann. Watch for new ones coming out and get on the special bonus email list and join Gary's fan page groups.

www.ingramcontent.com/pod-product-compliance
Lightning Source LLC
Chambersburg PA
CBHW081240280526
45787CB00006B/2742